Conversations
With
J. Krishnamurti

Conversations
With
J. Krishnamurti

The Man and the Message

N. Lakshmi Prasad

*This publication made possible with
the assistance of the Kern Foundation*

The Theosophical Publishing House
Wheaton, Ill. U.S.A.
Madras, India/London, England

A publication of the Theosophical Publishing House,
a department of the Theosophical Society in America

Library of Congress Cataloging-in-Publication Data

Prasad, N. Lakshmi, 1927–
    Conversations with J. Krishnamurti : the man and the message /
N. Lakshmi Prasad. –– 1st ed.
        p.   cm.
    Contains six interviews conducted in English from January, 1981
to December 1985, originally published in Telugu in two weekly
newspapers, Andhra Prabha and Andhra Jyoti, translated back
into English by the author for this work.
    "This publication is made possible with the assistance of the Kern
Foundation."
    "A Quest original"––Verso t.p.
    ISBN 0-8356-0661-9 (alk. paper)
    1. Krishnamurti, J. (Jiddu), 1895–   ––Interviews. 2. Philosophy.
I. Krishnamurti, J. (Jiddu), 1895–   . II. Title.
B5134.K754P72   1990
181'.4––dc20   90-50202
                                                                    CIP

Printed in the United States of America

Cover art by Brian Asimor

Dedicated to That which manifested
through J. Krishnamurti
during our time

Contents

Foreword

This is a collection of six interviews which Mr. Prasad had with Sri J. Krishnamurti between January, 1981, and December, 1985. These interviews are quite unique. Mr. Prasad's approach is much wider and he has probed into issues of life much deeper than the normal field of interest of popular magazines. Very few journalists would have been given the privilege of interviews with Krishnaji year after year.

Mr. Prasad, in the strict sense of the term, is not a journalist. He was asked to seek these interviews by the editor of the *Andhra Prabha Weekly* of Hyderabad because of his interest in the teachings of Krishnaji. He had attended Krishnaji's talks for many years and had read most of the published works. He was drawn to the charismatic personality of Krishnaji and wanted to meet him.

A perusal of the interviews will show the variety of topics covered and Mr. Prasad's capacity to bring out from Krishnaji some aspects of his teachings with clarity and simplicity.

In his question about scientific advancement, Krishnaji asks pointedly if science has helped man* to be good and moral. He points out that the scientists, while going into the nature and structure of matter, have "neglected research into the energy that does not constitute matter." They lack "a humanitarian approach." Talking about the future, he says that "if the present trend continues, then humanity has to face an atomic war."

In the same interview Krishnaji asks the question whether one can have a religion which is not based on belief, dogma, and ritual, but on a moral and ethical daily life. Can one come upon something sacred and live with that?

While talking about sensitivity, Krishnaji says that the brain is the center of the senses, and if we destroy the senses by control and suppression, we destroy the very brain. This does not mean that one pursues pleasure. If the heart cannot listen and enjoy something beautiful but dries up, how can it see beauty?

* In this book the term "man," used by Krishnamurti and the author, as well as Mr. Patwardhan, is meant to designate all of humankind.

On moral education and values, Krishnaji asks, "Will you teach the child to care for his neighbor, for his father and mother, for the trees and plants, for his surroundings? If there is love, care, and affection, there is morality."

His remarks about spreading his teachings are quite interesting. He says there is "no help to another in this direction." "The important thing is living the teachings and not their spreading."

I think these interviews are a valuable addition to the books on Krishnaji which have already been published.

P. H. Patwardhan,
former Secretary of the
Krishnamurti Foundation,
India

Preface

In 1971 I bought *The Penguin Krishnamurti
Reader* and tried to read it; it did not seem
to interest me, and it remained unread for
some time. Later in the year in a library, I
chanced upon one of the volumes of *Commentaries on Living*" by Sri Jiddu Krishnamurti,
which I read with interest. After that I avidly
got my hands on every book of Krishnamurti's
that was available in the libraries, bookstalls,
private collections of individuals, and read
them during all my spare hours after finishing
with my office work, sometimes far into the
night. Holidays were meant only for Krishnamurti reading, from which I derived great joy.
What is more, if I borrowed a Krishnamurti
book from someone, I had to write down
whole passages in my notebooks before I could
part with the book. Krishnamurti had gripped
me.

My boss during that period was Sri T.
Vedantam, I.A.S., Director of Census Opera-
tions, Hyderabad. (Incidentally, we were
classmates in college, and he was therefore a
friend in private.) He had an interest in

Krishnamurti's teaching and, noticing my serious interest, suggested that I go to Rishi Valley School for a few days when Krishnamurti would be there during December, 1972. This was extremely welcome, and I thanked him for the chance to meet Krishnamurti.

I also met Srimati Pupul Jayakar and Sri Achyut Patwardhan, who were in the valley. After some conversation, noticing my keen interest in Krishnamurti's teaching, they kindly invited me to lunch with him, along with some visitors. But formal introductions and buffet lunches with him did not satisfy me. I wanted to get in touch with him directly for a while, but I could not ask for a meeting just like that. Who would permit it? Long after, I told him that at that point I felt like scaling up the walls and barging into his room to talk to him. "Good, good," was his smiling response to this "impetuosity."

Every year thereafter, I attended his talks held in the South of India. For a decade I was unable to get close to him, though I had read almost every word of his that was published.

In the year 1980 my journalist friend, Sri Pothuri Venkateswara Rao, took charge as editor of the *Andhra Prabha Weekly,* a journal of long standing that was of considerable popularity in the Telugu land. He knew of my interest in Krishnaji; and since I had been a

freelance writer in Telugu for a fairly long
period, he suggested that I interview him for
the weekly. This presented the needed opportunity for me to get into touch with Krishnamurti. Naturally I took it up with alacrity.

The conversations contained in this book are
based on the notes taken by my wife and me
while Krishnamurti was replying to my
questions in a series of interviews. During the
course of one interview, Krishnamurti asked
me what I did with all that I was getting from
him. I told him that my wife and I wrote
down whatever he said and later pieced it
together carefully. I then translated it
diligently, carrying the spirit of it into the
Telugu language before giving it for
publication.

"Why don't you use a tape recorder? I have
a beautiful tape recorder over there in the
room," Krishnaji suggested.

I replied unhesitatingly, "No, I don't want a
tape recorder. I want this interview only in
this manner." My intention was that the
atmosphere during the interview be totally
informal and not artificial. A tape recorder
would, therefore, not suit my purpose. Krishnamurti understood and nodded with a smile.

In a teaching life spanning over seven
decades, Krishnamurti has addressed thou-

sands of people and must have given an understanding of life to at least some of those who were earnest. But each one of us can receive from him only according to our own measure.

Acknowledgments

I want to thank the publishers of *Añdhra Prabha* and *Añdhra Jyoti* weekly newspapers, in which these interviews originally appeared in Telugu, for consenting to have the English version published in this book. Thanks also to Sri M. A. Hamid in Rishi Valley, who obliged me with photographs of Krishnamurti for publication in the journal as well as in this book.

I am grateful to P. H. Patwardhan, former Secretary of the Krishnamurti Foundation, India, for kindly writing the foreword. My thanks are also due to his brother, Sri Achyut Patwardhan, one-time Socialist leader of great repute and a close associate of Krishnamurti for decades (see footnote in Interview 3), who participated in two of the interviews. Thanks also go to Dr. Sunanda Patwardhan and Dr. Radhika Herzberger, who kindly arranged the interviews at Madras. Sri G. Narayan and Mrs. Thomas helped me in regard to the meetings at Rishi Valley.

I also want to thank my wife, Srimati
Damayanti, without whose encouragement
and cooperation I would not have been able to
do all this work. She herself is a keen student
of Krishnamurti's teachings and occasionally
speaks in Telugu on the All India Radio,
Hyderabad, touching on their relevance to the
problems of women. I thank my son-in-law,
Dr. S. P. Uma Rao, Assistant Professor in
the University of Southwestern Louisiana, for
preparing the ground and putting me in touch
with the intelligentsia and the publishers of
this book in the United States.

I thank the Theosophical Publishing House
for bringing out this book, and I am deeply
grateful to its senior editor, Mrs. Shirley
Nicholson, for the consistent encouragement
that she gave me in this regard.

Introduction:
Awakening the Whole Man

Academicians and thinkers generally tend to
divide knowledge into various disciplines—
physics, mathematics, economics, sociology
and psychology. But Jiddu Krishnamurti, the
noted thinker, educationist, and philosopher,
does not deal with these branches of knowledge separately. He takes them all together
and talks about something behind all these
apparent divisions of knowledge. Similarly in
the field of fine arts, one finds that Krishnamurti does not talk about music, dance,
drama separately but lumps them together
and talks of something which is perhaps the
source and mainspring of all the fine arts.

Thus Krishnamurti seems to deny the validity
of the intellect, which people think is man's
most precious tool for the development of
science, technology, and the progress of
humanity. Krishnamurti, however, does not
deny the utility of the intellect in achieving all
this but says that all this progress has not
solved the basic problem relating to the
agony, the loneliness and the psychological
uncertainty with which man continues to be

1

afflicted. However, the heart, the feeling instrument with its whole gamut of emotions, is not an adequate tool for solving the human problem, which requires something more than the intellect and the heart.

Krishnamurti then leads us on from the muddy waters of confused thinking and the turbulent emotions of an unknowing heart to a clear area of light and clarity where one sees without the physical eye and hears without the physical ear. Teachers have appeared on the world scene occasionally, but most of them have talked about *what* to think. Krishnamurti appears to be the only teacher who teaches humanity *how* to think, and then to discard thought to discover something new. A new faculty transcending the mere thinking-feeling-experiencing capacity of man is discovered, and this faculty when fully awakened cuts across all divisions, classifications, and compartmentalizations, to view the human problem wholly or holistically. Man, who is already divided according to race and language, has chosen to divide himself still further as the thinking man, the feeling man, the wise and the ignorant, the great and the small. All this divisive thinking is discarded by Krishnamurti, and man and life are viewed as a whole.

Man the world over is in constant conflict both inwardly and outwardly, and this is a cardinal, indisputable fact. He might escape physical suffering if he is lucky, but no man has ever been born who has escaped psychological suffering. Krishnamurti says there can be an end to this psychological suffering, a freeing of oneself from this enormous burden of sorrow so that one can look around for something sacred in life. To discover the sacred, if there is the sacred, is the call of Krishnamurti to the thinking perceptive individual. He invites you to participate in this joyous adventure wholeheartedly.

Interview 1
Vasanta Vihar, Madras
January, 1981

THIS INTERVIEW was conducted in the
first floor drawing room of Vasanta Vihar,
headquarters of the Krishnamurti Foundation,
India, at Adyar, Madras. Present with me
was my daughter Padmapriya, then a college
student, who had accompanied me because
she was keen to see the person whose writings
she had read extensively. Also present was
Achyut Patwardhan, former Socialist leader
and a close associate of Krishnamurti. (See
footnote in Interview 3.)

I believe I am the first person to insist that
Krishnamurti speak a few words in his native
tongue, Telugu, after speaking English for a
long, long time, perhaps for decades. This
was, of course, done in fun, but Krishnaji
obliged sportingly.

The last question as to why men merely worship those who break new ground, and will
not themselves undertake the task brought me
into real contact with Krishnamurti. Readers
will find his answer interesting.

Strife

Prasad: One notices so much strife at
present between communities and individuals,
both here and elsewhere. How do you see it?

J.K.: How do I see it? This conflict between man and man starts right at the individual level, within the family itself. There is no understanding even between the family members of the same household. Each is out for himself, with his or her own ambitions, dreams, and aspirations. Whatever you see in the family is found also in community life. It begins with the individual in the family, which later extends to the community, and then to the nation. The conflict must be solved at the first level, the individual level, before we can proceed to the next.

Communications

Prasad: The rapid development of communications should have resulted in more understanding between the peoples of the world. Instead, one sees more ideological conflict. Have improvements in speed and technology brought about a decline in human values and a loss of tenderness? Why so?

J.K.: Yes, human values have declined, obviously. More worldliness, the desire for money, sex, and power have increased. But your question is why this should happen. Technology has made these things available to a larger number of people than hitherto.

Every politician is after power. Money and sex are primary, dominant factors in everyone's life. Add to this the quick communication.

Given this structure, what will a man do? What would you expect? We are technologically very advanced, but morally very backward. Though gurus may talk about values, they don't do anything about them. Organized religions also talk about them, but do nothing. The gurus are interested in power. They do not encourage you to inquire.

Prasad: They don't invite discussion . . .

J.K.: Gurus just lay down what is to be done. If you discuss, they are nowhere. The gurus try to build their power base. They are always estimating the numerical strength of their disciples.

And so—who is going to save man? Man will have to save himself.

Discipline

Prasad: While you welcome self-discipline, you are against all imposed discipline. But considering what is happening in this country today, would you desire the imposition of some discipline in all the various fields of activity, or would you not?

J.K.: Who is to teach whom? Are these corrupt governments in a position to teach people? Are the educational institutions in any better position to teach values to the students? Of course students take to drugs and destroy themselves. But the college professor gets his job through corrupt means. What example can such elders set for their students? The young ones see what their parents are doing, how they are living, what methods they adopt to rise in society. That is why we see this revolt, this rebellion on the part of the young.

So, boys and girls have to be given the right type of education; they have to understand right living. Begin at the school level.

Achyut Patwardhan (intervening): What he seems to suggest is that, as in a communist country, should there not be a ban on certain types of literature, etc., some discipline from the outside?

J.K.: Who taught me discipline? I was brought up in a particular way. No one told me that I should not drink, should not eat meat, should not smoke. Even so, I haven't done any of these things.

Achyut Patwardhan: There is one's own discipline, and the discipline that society imposes.

J.K.: Look what happens when someone starts imposing it, as in the Bhagalpur blindings. (Krishnaji is here referring to the deliberate blinding by the authorities of certain notorious robbers in prison custody, about which there was some publicity and consequent uproar.)

Prasad: But would you not restrain a madman?

J.K.: But if one who restrains a madman is also mad? Now what is discipline? Discipline is "to learn." One has to learn. Monks and certain sects and orders have had strict discipline imposed on them all along. What happened? Today they are being permitted to marry. Why, unless there was a demand from those quarters?

Two Generations

Prasad: You have probably talked to more than two generations and seen how they react to your words. Can you tell us the difference between the thirties and the eighties of this century? Was there more intensity earlier which we lost in the superficialities of the present?

J.K.: People then believed in ideals and in fighting for them. They would not hesitate to give their life for the ideal. Take the Spanish War—they fought fascism and later communism. We know that certain people were committed to an ideal, a belief.

Prasad: As in this country, where the freedom struggle was waged.

J.K.: Yes, the freedom movement. It is so in every country—first the ideals and then the fall. It is the same all over.

Now nobody believes in anything. The other day, the Pope in Rome was saying, "We must see that we have more faith in the Savior and the Church." What does it mean?

Prasad: One lacks faith and one has to strengthen it.

J.K.: Man today believes in nothing. The more serious you are, the more you think; the more human you are, the less you believe in anything. Unless you discover a thing by yourself, you don't believe in anything, however great. When you discover it, you don't need belief; nobody need inculcate faith in you.

Native Tongue

Prasad:　A personal question. A long time ago you must have spoken in your mother tongue, Telugu. If I now speak to you in that language, will you be able to understand? Can you speak a few words in Telugu for the benefit of our readers?

J.K.:　I am sorry. I can't speak that language now. The boy whom they took at that time was told, "Learn one language perfectly. Learn the universal language English." Of course, I can also speak French, Italian, Spanish, etc. But they expected me to speak to the world. I was brought up in the most aristocratic atmosphere among the best English-speaking people.

Prasad:　But I have to persist for the sake of my readers.

J.K.:　(Smiling) All right. Persist.

Prasad:　They might have suggested that you speak only English. And you might have learned and spoken only that language.

Achyut Patwardhan: He wants to know whether you have a trace of the Telugu language left in you.

J.K.: Perhaps I can count a few numbers.

Prasad: All right, Sir. Even that will do.

J.K.: (Haltingly) Okati, Rendu, Moodu, Na-lu-gu (Telugu numbers signifying *one, two, three, four*).

(Now he hesitates and says *five* in English and utters the equivalent of *six* in Italian, and laughs.) That is all. I have already slipped into Italian.

Digging to a Greater Depth

Prasad: Down the ages, a rare person comes along to dig a well, quench his thirst, and share the waters with others. He passes on, and his followers do not seem to do any fresh digging. The well dries up in due course, and the followers go to any length to build a shrine around it and worship it, but are not willing to take the trouble of digging. Is this the fate of mankind?

Achyut Patwardhan: A very good question.

J.K.:   (He looks at the interviewer's face un-
believingly, perhaps because he did not expect
this from a newspaper interviewer.) Yes, it is
a good question. (Searchingly) Did you frame
this question?

Prasad: Of course it is mine. I have read a
lot of Sufi literature, Jelaluddin Rumi, and a
host of others. When I talk to people, they say
"Look here, this man is talking Krishnamurti."

J.K.:   All right, all right, I see. (Goes into
himself.) Man has been taught to follow;
follow the footsteps of some great man or
other. Not only in the spiritual domain, but in
every sphere of activity. In the political,
scientific and artistic world also, this has been
the rule. One wants to follow a Picasso, a
Beethoven. Man has been trained and conditioned to follow. You find security and
comfort in following, and that is what you
want. We don't want to think for ourselves,
because we have been told what to think and
not how to think. The society around us, our
education, our religions have encouraged us to
conform, to imitate, to obey. For a thousand
years you have encouraged me to follow. My
brain resists everything else. What else can
I do?

That is how we are. Did you attend the meeting [where Krishnamurti spoke] yesterday?

15

Prasad: Yes sir, I was there.

J.K.: Even while I talked to so many yesterday and asked them to examine the issue along with me, they moved with me only a little, and then got lost on the way. That is how people are.

Prasad: We now take leave of you, sir.

At this point, my daughter Padmapriya, and I tried to move away.

Krishnamurti accompanied both of us down the stairs of Vasanta Vihar and said, ''Whenever I am here, and whenever you are here, you are welcome to see me, sir.''

I was originally given twenty minutes for the interview, but it went on for about forty-five minutes. Krishnaji, thereafter, was willing to treat me as a ''friend.''

Interview 2
Vasanta Vihar, Madras
December, 1981

THE FIRST interview with Krishnamurti ever published in the Telugu language, appeared in early 1981 in the *Andra Prabha Weekly,* along with a color photograph of him on the cover page and a number of smaller photographs on the inside pages. It drew tremendous response from the Telugu readers, and the editor was flooded with a large number of appreciative letters. The Secretary at Vasanta Vihar wrote to the editor, for copies of the issue, in order to send them to some of the Krishnamurti organizations. A dozen copies were furnished by the editor.

While the older generations of theosophists and the general public had known Krishnamurti for a fairly long time, the younger generation of the Telugu-speaking people knew practically nothing of him. After seeing the transcript of the interview, some took pride in his belonging to the Telugu land, though that was really inconsequential. Some were pained to see that Krishnaji had lost touch with his mother tongue altogether, though they were pleased to learn that he could count a few numbers in his native language. It would be naive to expect the average Telugu reader to rise above his language parochialism and pride, and see the fact that Krishnamurti was not only beyond all languages but was also beyond all thought, on which humanity generally prides itself.

When Srimati Sunanda Patwardhan, who had arranged the interview, told Krishnaji that the person who had earlier interviewed him during 1981 sought an interview for the second time, it appears he remarked, "Oh, that man with his daughter. All right." Reporting this to me, she joked, "Though he is against memories operating in man, when he wants to, he seems to remember things quite well."

Accompanied by my wife and daughter, I greeted Krishnamurti on the first floor of Vasanta Vihar on the day of the interview. He invited me to take a chair, while he sat cross-legged on the carpet. "We would feel happy to sit along with you," we said as we sat down on chairs. "Ah, but then what are these chairs for, if no one uses them?" he joked.

I put a copy of the typed questions before him. My family and I held other copies. This was to ensure that Krishnamurti's time was not wasted with irrelevancies and that we would not move away from the main points. I had a self-imposed obligation to my readers to draw out Krishnaji in respect to specific matters.

Krishnamurti looked at the sheet of typed questions and joked, "My annual examination paper, sir?" I countered with a feeble

21

joke. "But I worked harder at setting up the questions than you will while answering them."

Without the aid of glasses, even in his eighty-seventh year, Krishnamurti read each question and replied patiently. The advantage of having my wife and daughter with me to take notes simultaneously while Krishnamurti was speaking became evident later, when I had to make whole sentences of the words, phrases, and snatches of conversation spoken by him. All three of us knew only longhand in writing English. I was averse to using a tape recorder, which would introduce an element of artificiality in an otherwise spontaneous conversation. And yet there was the need for conveying whatever Krishnamurti communicated without distortion, without omission, and as truthfully as possible, except for elaborating a point here or there, which I did for the sake of structuring the answer in a proper sequence. The fact that I had studied practically all the available books and verbatim reports of Krishnaji's talks stood me in good stead and helped me to convey the whole thing, I hope, fairly precisely.

Science and Its Future

Prasad: Scientific advancement has turned out to be both beneficial and harmful. What is the future of science in the story of mankind?

J.K.:   But what is science? Development of science and the connected technological advance has produced great benefits for humanity. That is so. The advances made in surgery, medicine, and communications have helped humanity enormously. In agriculture and the biological sciences also there have been great advances. Some of this development is no doubt highly beneficial, but some of it is also destructive.

However, only some scientists and some scientific institutions are devoted to activity which increases human welfare. There are others willing to undertake research for destructive purposes at the instance of governments or some other institutions. This is how we see science. But what exactly is science? What is its precise meaning?

Prasad: One judges science only on the basis of the shape that it has assumed in the present age, whether it is beneficial or destructive.

J.K.:   What shape it has assumed is one thing, but what should be its purpose, what should be its outlook? Has science helped man to be good and moral, with a sense of the beautiful and the aesthetic? Has it conducted research into these aspects? Or has it only created new desires in man to confuse him further? What is science and what is the scientific outlook? Is it not to examine things without any opinion, without prejudgment, without prejudice, to discover facts? Is this not the scientific temperament? Scientists can then make use of these discoveries for the benefit of humanity. Is this not their duty?

Prasad: But the scientists seem to be under the impression that their duty is only to conduct research and discover the secrets of nature. They think that it is the lookout of the people and their governments as to how they use those discoveries.

J.K.: That is where they are mistaken. Science has concentrated its entire attention on energy as matter. In that process it has placed enormous destructive capacity in the hands of man. This was not the type of research that should have been encouraged. Why have the scientists neglected research into the energy that does not constitute matter? Why have they not been interested in that type of energy? This enormous energy could have been explored in all its ramifications, but why have they confined themselves to one part of energy that is found in the shape of matter? Why do the scientists lack a humanitarian outlook? Is science at fault? Or is it the scientists that are at fault? Or is it the fault of governments that encourage them to create these destructive instruments? If it is man that is to blame, why find fault with science as such?

Only the other day I was able to fly by jet plane at top speed from Frankfort to this place. . . .

Achyut Patwardhan: With the same type of machine one could also rain bombs on innocent people. Whether a thing is put to constructive or destructive use is thus entirely dependent on man.

J.K.: The question is, What is the role of science in the future of humanity? If the present trends continue, then humanity will have to face an atomic war. If human beings look around and see what is happening, they can decide how they are going to use science, and take steps accordingly. To say that one will learn through experience after an atomic war which will destroy the majority of mankind, and that the few left would then plan for the peaceful benefits of science, that is something else.

Scientists and governments interested in human welfare should be able to say now, not in the future, that they will cease manufacturing destructive weapons, and they should destroy the existing weapons straightaway. If this resolve is not made now, it will have to be done after the atomic holocaust by the very few survivors, if there are any left. Why not do it now? We are responsible for the whole thing, and we have to find out which is the wiser course.

Organized Religions: Aggressive Postures

Prasad: Established religions are becoming more and more aggressive in their postures and, in their attempt to extend their spheres of influence, are coming into conflict with one another, thus endangering the peace of the world. Is there a possibility of the saner elements coming together to avert this?

J.K.: Except for the Buddhist religion most of the religions are doing what you say. Religion today is big business. Some of the organized religions are doing it openly and blatantly with their big money and muscle power. Some other groups are doing it with only money power. To believe blindly in something, whatever it is, and then thrust it forcibly on others is all wrong. There is no need to discuss organized religions such as Islam and Christianity, whose activities are well known. But this sort of thing seems to have now crept into Hinduism also. These people have now started constructing temples in foreign towns and cities like New York, Milwaukee, and Philadelphia. Do you want to carry all this nonsense that is going on in the name of Hinduism over to those countries? Do you have to export all this to those foreign cities? What are you going to achieve by taking all this superstition, this pomposity, this gibberish to those places?

Religion, by and large, has lost its real content. It is today being organized like any other business house, any one of the huge corporations with their methods. Behind these organized religions, there are very strong forces operating. They have the money to spend and would not hesitate to use strong-arm methods. The newspapers also do not criticize them and are silent so far as their activities are concerned. Who would wish to criticize these organized religions and thus lose their readers? The organized religions and the gurus are interested only in building up the strength of their institutions and the number of their followers. Is all this religion? Or is it mere fanaticism? And what is the difference between such religions and politics?

Your question is whether sane people can come together to avert the danger posed by these religions. But there are very few sane religious people. Sanity does not go with superstition. There is corruption all over and the so-called religious people are contributing to it. Look at the followers of these gurus quarreling with each other saying, "My guru is much better than yours." Where are the sane people? Can you find them amidst these competing groups?

And the intellectuals. They will have nothing to do with religion. They are shy of the very word "religion." They would rather not touch it. They do not seem to have inquired at all whether there is anything sacred, untouched by man, and whether it is possible to discover it. When one looks at all this, one wants to know whether one can have a religion which is not based on belief, dogma, ritual, but on a moral, ethical daily life. Can one come upon something sacred and live with that?

But who will listen?

Is Truth Only for the Few?

Prasad: You declare that your teaching is not for the select few but for the many.

28

Though you have been eager to give it to the many, as you have done all along, equality of opportunity has not resulted in equality of attainment. Only the few seem to benefit, and this has been so all through the history of mankind. Why?

J.K.: Isn't it difficult to break a habit? One falls into a pattern, a kind of lethargy, and then thinks, "What does it all matter?" People tend to become bitter and cynical. Very few want to be free, psychologically speaking. Man would like to be free outwardly, to do what he likes, but I am talking about freedom inside oneself. This demands exploration into oneself, a lot of hard work and thought. To break the old pattern requires tremendous energy.

The people who come to my meetings, wherever I speak, most come out of curiosity. How many of them want to lead a good, moral life? How many of them come to understand the whole thing and say, "I will work it out in my life. I will experiment with it and lead a good life"? The whole modern tendency is materialistic. People are only interested in money. Money has become god in this country, as football in Europe.

The word "good" has become old fashioned. To be good is to be holistic, not to be in contradiction within oneself. But life is so much under pressure, and one gets caught in it. How am I then to be good? There is this pressure of overpopulation. Physical survival itself is a problem in this country. How is one to teach goodness to a man under such tremendous pressure?

Only a few are interested in Truth. Unless one is able to go beyond all this and see that there is something important to find out, one gets trapped by the past. Most people do not want to find out. They just want entertainment. Even religion has become an entertainment. I was once going from Bombay to Delhi by train, and there were a few businessmen in my compartment, all busy people. One of them requested that I entertain them with my talk.

Prasad (in shocked disbelief):   They wanted you to entertain them?

J.K.:   Yes. That was what they wanted. That is how people are. These religious sects, gurus, disciples—all this has become just plain entertainment. Entertain people, build up a following, become powerful—this is what they are aiming at. Only a few are interested in the real thing, really earnest about it. What can one do? One can only sow the seed, and as they say, hope that it falls on good soil instead of stony terrain.

Words Come Alive

Prasad: After having read and listened to you, I found to my surprise that when I read any religious text of old, portions of it with an authentic ring stand out. I seem to have received the master key from you, and it enables me to open many a door of man's experience, religious or otherwise. Strange, or not so strange?

J.K.: That is what you seem to have felt. Some others, such as devout Catholics, have told me that they were reminded of Jesus Christ. Others have told me that this was what the Buddha said. If one is anchored in Christianity or Buddhism or Hinduism, one hears one's own prophet or God in those words. What you are saying is, of course, something different.

Prasad: I seem to have stated my personal experience but not to have framed my question properly.

J.K.: Whatever it is, shall we close this matter here and move to the next question?

Speaking While Meditating

Prasad: Across the span of time, one sees that the few who have been touched by this "ecstasy" have generally been bowled over, incapable of directing the steps of others. Your "controlled excitement," on the other hand, perhaps was intended to enable a larger number to harvest the golden crop?

Achyut Patwardhan (intervening): What is this controlled excitement? What does it mean?

J.K.: The words may not be conveying what he intends to say, but what he seems to mean is . . .

Achyut Patwardhan: How can you call a sense of profundity "excitement"? And what does controlled excitement mean?

Prasad: Many who have seen "That" were awe-struck. They practically turned God-mad and stuttered when they tried to speak. Words failed them. They were unable to share their experience fully with others. They then felt that there was nothing more to do in this world. But you speak even while you are in a state of deep meditation.

J.K.: I understand what you are saying. But instead of calling it controlled excitement we

32

will put it another way. Let us say that one is passionate about something. When you are really passionate about it, there is no need for excitement. The passion is burning, like a fire. Those who want to use it can make use of it, and those who do not want to do so remain aloof.

Putting it slightly differently, take a river with a large volume of water behind it. The flow of this water is controlled for the utility of man by building dams and projects across the river. But water, being water, because of its nature is rebelling. It wants to flow uninterruptedly. Water remains the same from the beginning to the end. Some use it, some don't.

Simple Words

Prasad: I have listened to you. I have read you through. There is never a difficult or complex word. If sometimes a not-so-simple word crops up while you speak, it is quickly noticed and dropped. A little conscious effort must be going into this?

J.K.: I will be very simple about it. When I go out to talk I haven't a single thought. If I use a wrong word while talking, I don't correct it immediately. I only investigate. Say,

33

for instance, what is the brain and what is the mind? What is the difference between the two? In investigating the difference, there is no effort involved. If I have to change the word, I do it. In a discussion, if someone suggests a more precise word, I accept it.

Simple words are much more direct than complex words. Using simple words is not an art that I have practiced as such. Of course, Mrs. Besant [who raised K. and saw to his education] told me when I was young to read the Old Testament. It is possible that this might be influencing me to some extent while I talk. But for that matter, any language is best spoken only in simple words. Such words go directly to the heart of the listener. No one can create complex or distorted meanings for such words. One can listen and understand directly.

Senses

Prasad: Man attempts to do something good and finds himself impeded for one reason or another. Could this be the result of some action of his stretching back into the unknown past?

J.K.: Why do you say "unknown past"? Look at the community around and notice its

34

indifference, its lack of intelligence and sensitivity. This is the impediment. Our religious leaders are partly responsible for this. They insist on the destruction of man's senses. This is an error. The brain is the center of the senses, and if you destroy the senses, you destroy the very brain.

Of course, sense indulgence is harmful, but are we going to destroy the senses on that account? If one wants to see the beauty of this world, the senses have to operate properly. If you destroy them altogether because of the risk of indulgence involved, will it not lead to more harm?

Suppose you lose your sense of beauty? Then you will not be able to see and enjoy a beautiful flower. It is only when you want to pluck out the plant from the ground and put it in your own backyard that the conflict begins. Otherwise what harm is there in looking at the flower and enjoying it? If the heart cannot listen and enjoy something beautiful but dries up, how can it ever see beauty? All the senses will have to flower.

If you suppress and thereby destroy the senses, even the mind will become dull. It will lose its sensitivity and become hard and rigid. This has to be examined carefully by religious leaders. The gurus, being unable to discover truth, are satisfied with words and symbols and teach the same thing to their disciples. Words and symbols have thus become substitutes for action.

Conflict between the Good and Bad

Prasad: Apparently wrongdoers seem to prosper while those who are principled continue to suffer in this world. Any explanation?

J.K.: Who is a wrongdoer? What do you call bad? How many are really good? If the so-called good is the opposite of bad, it is not good. It is the sort of good born out of the bad. Real good is beyond the opposites of bad and good. Such a really good person will be whole, without division. He will not say one thing, do something else, and think in an entirely different manner. What he thinks, he says, and what he says, he does.

What is generally found in the world is the so-called good which is just the opposite of bad, born as reaction to bad. This sort of good springs from thought and it comes out of fear, the fear of society. This good hankers after recognition from society and is disappointed when it does not get it. It is ridden with conflict and therefore of no value. Any good that thought conjures up will have the seeds of bad within it.

But there is no opposite for real goodness. If it wants to do something, it does it without thought of the consequences. Whatever it has discovered for itself, whatever it really loves, it does it, whatever others think.

Indian Culture: Degeneration

Prasad: Successive foreign invasions and foreign rule have not destroyed Indian culture as speedily as have thirty-five years of self-rule. How did this happen?

J.K.: I have been coming to this country almost every year. Its culture seems to be deteriorating year after year. It is not I alone who should be concerned about it, but all of you.

At one time there was order in this country based on fear. Fear ruled; people were afraid to misbehave or fight among themselves. Now no one is afraid. The moment you remove fear, people start behaving as they please.

Seven centuries of Muslim rule has not made a serious dent in this culture. Even one and a half to two centuries of British rule has not been able to destroy this culture except for a little. But just with thirty-five years of self rule. . .

Achyut Patwardhan: When confronted with the foreign foe, the best in the people came up to fight the enemy. In their battle with the foreigner, people were naturally thrown back on their ancient culture, to which they looked for sustenance and strength. They therefore preserved and nurtured it carefully.

But today people are unable to recognize the internal foe which is destroying us. Freedom has enabled the internal enemy to surface. Unless we see clearly that what is really destroying our culture today is this internal enemy, this lack of direction and the fact that we are the very cause of our downfall. . .

J.K.: Look at what happened as soon as fear was removed. Why has the culture of this country broken up? How did they manage to destroy it within such a short period? Why have the moral values gone down so badly? Is it that the Indian culture does not have inherent strength in it? Or is it that the foreign administration was able to instill fear and thus enforce discipline among the people? Is there any place for merit in this country? Is there anyone who recognizes honesty and efficiency? Or do the efficient and intelligent have to migrate to the West? When I talk to

38

those who have settled there, they tell me that they are able to do whatever they love to do, and are doing well both professionally and financially.

Are they giving real education in the Indian universities? Is there encouragement for the classical arts, or is it for cheap dance and music?

Achyut Patwardhan: While we are very interested in tapping the natural resources of the country and improving the living standards of the people, which is all to the good, are we equally interested in developing our human resources, in improving the character and the skills of the people, or are we neglecting these things altogether?

J.K.: Within a period of just three and a half decades you have been able to tear to shreds the culture of over three thousand years. You have destroyed the matrix, the very base of this country. What should happen in the future? If everyone is interested only in money and power, what should happen to the children born to all of you? Have you ever thought of this? You just worship some gods on the hilltops, recite something from the so-called sacred books, and carry on. What should one think of your gurus and their blind followers? If those who have some vision, some foresight, do not come together and think over what is happening all around, what will happen to this country and its culture?

"I Do Not Belong to Any Class."

Prasad: Your life style conforms to the upper middle class. How can a person, worried and anxious about the daily necessities of life, take to your teaching?

J.K.: Why do you call it upper middle class? It is perhaps even above that. I go from one place to another by air. Within each country I use someone's car for travel. But this I don't do for fun. Just as all of you look forward to my visit in this country, there are others in other countries who await my visit every year. Actually, it is not good for one's health to move at such speed from one country to another.

What I wear in this country (showing a piece of the cloth of his shirt) is rather cheap material. You might not have seen the type of suits I wear in the Western countries. They are made of much costlier material, much more expensive. But I am not interested in these clothes. My friends bear my travel expenses. Whatever is needed for keeping this body alive is given by friends. Whatever they give me, I wear. Whatever they put before me, I eat. This I have been doing for over fifty years.

"Middle class" would signify that one earns, or that one has some unearned income. But I have no money at all. I don't have a bank account. Wherever I go, I don't ask for anything except for a little shelter, a little food, and some clothes to wear. I don't smoke or drink or eat meat; I have never done any of these things. For that matter I have no habits at all. I have been working all my life. To enable me to work like this, friends keep supporting me.

Mentally I am not middle class. In fact, I do not belong to any class; I hope not.

You ask how a man struggling for daily necessities can take interest in my teaching. Each one has his own problems. One would have to solve them at their respective levels. I am not saying that those matters should be neglected. But the problems that man faces in the world are of one variety, while the conflict that he faces within himself is of a different character. For problems at one level there are solutions at that level. But we add psychological conflict to those problems and make them extremely complex. Even those people who seem to have solved their economic problems are not able to solve their psychological problems.

What I am saying is that there is a way out of this psychological conflict and the resultant sorrow, and that one can go beyond this to find something sacred. It is up to him. Nobody can compel him. There is no point in moralizing. It is for him to discover. It will bring peace and joy. It will also set right the things of the world. If you are interested, I am asking you to discover that.

Interview 3
Rishi Valley
December, 1982

BEFORE HE arrived in Rishi Valley in December, 1982, Krishnamurti spoke at Calcutta, the capital city of West Bengal, where a communist government was in power. I could not ask Krishnaji for his reactions to the meeting at Calcutta, since politics is a subject in which he took no interest. I therefore approached his long time associate Sri Achyut Patwardhan* and sought his reactions to those meetings.

Prasad: This is perhaps the first time that Krishnamurti addressed public meetings in Calcutta, under a communist government. How did the people receive his talks?

Achyut Patwardhan: To all four talks held in Calcutta, people came in thousands. They heard him perhaps more carefully than in the other towns.

Prasad: The people there have a different political ideology and an atheistic outlook—

* The seventy-seven year old Sri Achyut Patwardhan was one of the founders of the Congress Socialist Party during the struggle for India's freedom. Standing shoulder to shoulder with national leaders like Mahatma Gandhi, Jawaharlal Nehru, and Jayaprakash Narayan, Sri Patwardhan had struggled untiringly for India's liberation and the establishment of a socialist society. During the "Quit India" movement of 1942, he went underground and played a prominent role in running a "parallel government" in areas of the Maharashtra

wasn't this a hindrance to understanding Krishnaji's teaching?

Achyut Patwardhan: From the questions that people in Calcutta put to him, one could see that Krishnamurti's talk provoked a lot of thinking among them. When the country was under the foreign yoke, was it not the Bengalis who first took up the cause of cultural regeneration and political revolution? They have the spirit to endure hardship for what they believe in, and they even die for it if necessary. When they felt that the removal of economic disparities could be effected only through the Marxist ideology, they took to that path. But when they saw what happened in the communist countries all over the world, and the chasm that developed between the theory and practice of the communist regimes, they grew disillusioned. The need for taking a fresh look at all ideologies, political and economic, has now become extremely urgent. What can one do for man's real welfare and

state, even while the British were ruling the country.

Achyutji was one of those who believed that Indian independence, ushered in during 1947, would change the face of the country, but was sadly disillusioned by the type of politics that emerged in post-independent India. He therefore abandoned active politics after some time and devoted himself to the regeneration of human values. In this endeavor he came closer to Krishnamurti with whom he had been associated even earlier, and has worked with him since.

real freedom? is the crucial question at this
moment. Krishnaji has been able to take this
inquiry forward by a few more steps.

At least some would carry this inquiry further.
The seeds that Krishnaji has sown may find
fertile soil at least in some minds. Whoever
considers life's problems seriously is sure to
find Krishnamurti's words extremely relevant.

Prasad: Some people look at all human
problems only from the economic angle. Are
they likely to find any meaning in Krishnaji's
teaching?

Achyut Patwardhan: It is a fact that all of
us once believed that the key to all of man's
problems lay in the removal of poverty from
our midst. So we worked for it incessantly.
But one is led to doubt whether man will
really improve even after he gets rid of his
poverty. Instead of drinking cheap liquor, he
might perhaps take to whiskey. If he was subject to exploitation earlier, in his new role he
might take to exploiting another. Poverty is
not merely economic in nature. If one is poor
in regard to his morals and character, then
such poverty brings the human being to a
very low level. While directing one's effort to
the removal of poverty in the economic field,
one should simultaneously work for moral regeneration and the establishment of ethical
values. The freedom of our country, which is

the result of countless sacrifices on the part of many, will be worthwhile only if we are able to achieve such a society.

Thinkers who can uncover and show us the state to which we are reduced and then activate us have always appeared on the scene when the country needed them. They sow the new seed. Such men do not ask for the adulation. They only expect people to listen to them and change their lives for the better. People should patiently try to understand what Krishnaji is telling them and should not wait for leaders to come and lead them. But they should act with sincerity and earnestness.

This time the venue of our meeting with Krishnamurti was the open hall on the first floor of the old guest house at Rishi Valley School. Krishnamurti came out of his room and greeted my family and me in the open hall and sat down on the carpet, asking us to sit on the cushions. Krishnaji looked at my daughter, Padmapriya, and was reminded of his previous offer to her to come to Rishi Valley and teach. "You aren't coming here?" he asked. I intervened to say she intended to do her post graduate work. Krishnaji laughed, "What for? A commerce degree and then an M.B.A.? Don't you intend to come here? Would you not like it?" Padmapriya replied, "I would love to be here." Krishnamurti looked at her for a while and said "With your parents' approval, of course." Padmapriya joined the Rishi Valley School as a teacher in January, 1984.

Science and Superstition

Prasad: The advances made in scientific knowledge should have resulted in less superstition. Instead, one notices strange cults and cheap magic becoming more and more popular. Can you suggest the reason, sir?

J.K.: Science has not helped man except technologically. It has resulted in better transport, bigger bathrooms, better hygiene, medicinal advances, new communication media. It also sustains war, and thus the world is in chaos. Standards of living have improved, but human life has been placed in greater danger with the invention of terrible weapons of war.

Looking at all this, man does not know what to do. People run after comfort. They seek some escape from all this. They then follow some crooked guru who makes money off them. The gurus with their cheap magic deceive their followers and convince them that it is possible to escape all this misery and terror through some trick or other. The gurus do not hesitate to mislead their followers for the sake of personal gain.

The politicians are no better. They do not provide any security to ordinary people. Therefore any phony thing goes. The people are willing to catch at anything and hang on to it for mental comfort and security. Hence the increase in tribal gods and superstitions. Look at the way in which the gurus and their followers are constructing temples in the United States.

See how people escape from their basic problems through sports and other activities. Sport, which should have simply been the happy expression of human playfulness, has today become a big industry. See how they are organizing it. Drugs and sex attract people in a greater measure. And with all this, more gods. Whoever comes up with a new trick promising salvation has people willing to follow him. So long as people run after illusory things and do not try to find out what is essential in their lives, things will be the same as now.

Man's Nature

Prasad: Is man's original nature good or bad? Are there innate dispositions in him that shape him into a good or bad person?

J.K.: Biologists, scientists, and anthropologists have said that man has evolved from the ape. If you accept that, then he has come through a lot of violence. In addition to the violence that he has thus acquired through this animal ancestry, man has also learned to wage organized war. Any historian will tell you about the thousands of wars fought through human history. Everyone knows that war is the most terrific calamity that could happen to humanity, and yet it goes on, with the aid of new weapons, more modern than those of yesterday. Everyone knows that killing is wrong. They say it in books. But have they stopped killing? No. We have all the problems inherited from the animal, and added to them specific human problems, saying one thing and doing another.

The battle between the so-called good and bad goes on endlessly. You put the saint on one side and the devil on the other, and then write or paint of the good waging a battle with the bad. Even primitive man seems to have conceived of good and bad and painted pictures on caves showing the good interlocked with the bad in a fierce battle. But does this duality exist at all? Man considers that the good is the opposite of the bad. But if the so-called good is the outcome of evil, then it is not good. Such "good" has the seeds of bad in it, and at a later date it will turn out to be bad in a different context.

Take the man who says he is practicing nonviolence. He seeks violence and then reacts to it by positing a so-called ideal of nonviolence. But such nonviolence is only a suppression of the violence inside the person. It is just bottled up. This opposite of violence is a mere construct of thought and has no value. Violence is the fact, and nonviolence is an idea. It is violence that has to be dealt with, because that is what is. Once you are free of violence, you are utterly different.

Prasad: Is there not relative good and bad?

J.K.:   No. Real good has no relationship to the bad. Such real good is totally divorced from evil. Real good is beyond both the so-called good and evil. The man who discovers such good is the really good man. He has no conflict.

Man Everywhere Is the Same

Prasad: Is the substance in each person the same except that it is differently organized?

J.K.: What do you mean by essence, substance? Some Christians interpret it one way and the fundamentalists in another way. People in America are going back to the Bible.

But the consciousness of mankind is the same all over. Man everywhere has the same fears, the same anxiety, and the same pain. His superstitions, his blind faith, his sorrow, his feeling of insecurity, his seeking of pleasure are common features. Consciousness basically is the same in all mankind. We share the same ground. Depending upon the time in which one lives and the circumstances that a man faces, there may be some superficial differences. But your consciousness is not different from mine. Thought born out of this consciousness, is the same. Thinking is the same, whether it is that of the farmer in the field or of the scientist in the lab. So one can say that man thinks, but there is nothing like "your thinking" and "my thinking." Depending upon the country in which a man is born, the circumstances and the society in which he is brought up, the experiences that he has undergone, and his education, he thinks in a certain way. But that does not mean that his thinking is unique to himself. Thinking, wherever it occurs, is just thinking. You behave in a certain way because you grew up under certain conditions and had a certain set of experiences. I behave differently because of some other experiences and conditioning. Environmental pressures and influences happen to be different. What one likes, the other doesn't. That's the difference, a difference on the periphery.

You have a high position in society. You have knowledge. You are treated with respect by everyone. They flatter you. Since I am an ordinary man, I have none of these things. Then your behavior is different from mine.

Prasad: And if both of us are plain, ordinary men?

J.K.: You may not be greedy, and I may be utterly greedy. You have no ambition and therefore no intention to compete, but I am, say, very competitive. You are gentle, because you are not attached. I am attached. In that case, our behavior is bound to be different. But if you are able to find right action in life, then it is right for you and me. It will influence us similarly. There is no difference between you and me when we lead a life of righteousness. We do not do good to some and bad to others. It is good for both of us, for all of us.

Serious about Life

Prasad: Why is this "deep thirst" a felt need only for the few?

J.K.: You mean by that, Why are some people serious while others are not? First of all, why do we divide ourselves like this? Why are we not affectionate and loving towards each other? Why do we fight each other, develop enmity, and enlarge our differences? Do you see how miserable we have become on account of all this?

Man is chiefly interested in comfort and pursuit of pleasure and wants to be entertained. This is perhaps the reason for lack of seriousness. But if you look around, who is really serious? Are the politicians serious? Are the local leaders serious? Are the rich serious? Alternatively, are the poor serious? How many are really serious in life?

Even if someone like me comes along and says, "Look at life seriously," they will respond with, "How well spoken, how true!" and then carry on as usual. That is all. Praise the man and be finished with him. They then fall back into their routine, their old ways. Does anybody say, "We need not agree with what he says, but we will find out whether what he is saying is true"? How many of them have this sort of energy? The Buddha spoke for forty years. Of those who heard him carefully, only two are said to have understood him. And even those two passed away before Buddha did! Look at the tragedy of the whole thing.

"I Am Humanity"

Prasad: Will you kindly elucidate your statement, "I am humanity, not the collective"?

J.K.: We are all human beings, and we have to be treated as such. But men are being treated in society as the mass; they are viewed collectively. They are sacrificed for some ideology. This is happening everywhere. This is not the way to look at a human being. He has to be understood at the individual level. One must find a solution at the individual human level. If you treat human beings as a herd, as the collective, and use them for political or economic or some other selfish purpose, you are doing wrong.

Now, take this school in Rishi Valley. There are about twenty children per class. Compared to other schools, this is very few. Even so, I have suggested that the number be reduced to twelve per class. They are moving in that direction. My intention is that there

should be greater care and attention to each
student by the teacher. Only then would the
teacher be able to help the student to flower.

If you treat man in the collective, you can't
have compassion; you can't be gentle. You
are likely to become indifferent and harsh.
When I see the truth that my consciousness is
the consciousness of all human beings, I can
treat a person only as a human being, and not
in the mass. Do you now understand why
I say that I am humanity?

Human Consciousness

Prasad: You say, "If one single human
being understands fear radically and resolves
it, he affects the whole consciousness of mankind." How does resolution in one case affect
the rest of mankind? Has it ever happened?

J.K.: You will have to understand that consciousness of human beings is the same all
over. If that which is bad can influence
human consciousness, the good can also have
an influence. You know how men like Hitler
and Stalin affected the consciousness of their
people. You also know how the good ones
affected the consciousness of mankind. The
Buddha influenced the whole of the East during his time. That is why I say that even if

one person were to completely understand his fear and drop it, then he would be able to affect the consciousness of mankind.

Prasad: What Hitler and Stalin did was to whip up the passions of their people and generate hatred against others. That is relatively easy. What has that to do with a good man's work, which is an uphill task?

J.K.: It is just that very few want to go in this direction. If you step out of the stream and a few others do likewise, everything may change. This is a fact, not a sentimental theory.

Prasad: Has it happened?

J.K.: That you can't judge. Each has to decide for himself.

I will tell you something about experiments conducted into the group consciousness of rats. Researchers in America and Australia took up these experiments in their respective countries independently, without any consultation or interchange of ideas. They had huge boxes made with light on one side and darkness on the other. If the rat went towards the lighted end, he got an electric shock. If he went towards the dark side, he got food. Thus a system of punishment and reward was instituted.

M. A. Hamid, Rishi Valley, India

When one rat discovered this and understood what it meant, he naturally went only towards darkness and avoided the lighted end. What one rat in the group knew, the other rats seemed to grasp intuitively, and they acted in a similar manner within a short while. What one rat knows doesn't need an entire generation to be transmitted to its progeny as in the case of genetics. Through the functioning of the group consciousness, it is speedily transmitted to the other rats around it.

The scientists conducted these experiments not merely on one generation of rats, but on twenty-five generations. I am not talking of the genetic aspect; I am speaking about the speed with which the knowledge of one rat is transmitted to its group. The fact is that scientists in America and Australia conducted these experiments separately and found that the results were the same and that group consciousness is affected in a similar manner all over.

Whether this is sufficient proof in respect to humans or not, it is obvious that one man's consciousness and conduct influences the persons around him. That is indisputable. If man's consciousness can be affected in such a manner as to take the wrong direction, then it can equally be affected to take the right direction.

Even if a few stand aside, then our social consciousness can be given a different direction. But where are the people who would like to move in this direction? How many are willing to step out of the mainstream of society?

Helping Another

Prasad: One can help another person to be aware only if that person is a little aware already. Otherwise, one can only hope that in due course the other person will come to it of his own accord. Please comment.

J.K.: Why do you think you are starting out to help me? And at what level do you want to help me? First of all, are you aware? If you are not aware, do not talk about awareness. If there is no awareness in you and you start talking about awareness to me, that is plain hypocrisy. If you are aware, will I not be able to see it in you? Will I not see how you behave towards your wife, children, servants, friends, and all the others? If you live with awareness, will I not be able to notice it? Any change that has to take place will then take place in me. You need not do anything. Your manner, your attitude, your conduct, your talk will all reveal to me everything that I have to know. It will, of course, depend upon how well I grasp it.

Prasad: One should set an example?

J.K.: No, no. One does not go about deliberately setting an example.

Prasad: That was not what I meant. The conduct of a man who is aware is seen by others and understood, which enables them to change themselves.

J.K.: Ah, that's right.

Awakened Intelligence

Prasad: Does the awakened intelligence expand? Does it become deeper? Otherwise, a long life has no meaning.

J.K.: What is important is the awakening of intelligence. Intelligence has no expansion or contraction. If it has expansion and contraction and is measurable, then it is not intelligence. Intelligence is not cultivated by thought. Intelligence is born through insight. This intelligence is not craftiness, cleverness, nor accumulation of knowledge. It has no relation to thought. The ability to build bridges, projects, machines, and computers is different. The accumulation of knowledge and the capacity born out of it is not the awakening of intelligence.

This is an intelligence born of insight. When this intelligence is awakened, compassion is born. All the other capacities will have to act in accordance with this compassion. Compassion has its own intelligence.

Prasad: If intelligence is once awakened and does not grow, then what is the purpose of living thereafter?

J.K.: When intelligence is awakened, compassion comes into being. Compassion does not mean joining some religious group. If I become a Catholic or Hindu and am anchored there and do some social work, that is not being compassionate.

Compassion does not come through thought. It does not make a distinction between you and another. Once this compassion comes into being, can fear and suffering continue? Can duality find place in the compassionate one? Will he think of either his life or death? Unless there is some dissatisfaction, some lack of fulfillment, some anxiety, will this thought about living and dying arise at all? If you live completely and wholly, will you think of life or death at all? Fear always haunts the mind that chews on its memories and is anxious for the future. If this fear of the "me" and "mine" is dropped completely, where is the question of one state being desirable and something else being undesirable? At that point, what difference is there between living and dying? Life in freedom will be a life of compassion.

Teacher and the Taught

Prasad: You deny "the teacher and the taught." But there is an unfolding which occurs when you speak which clarifies the issues.

J.K.: If I say that when you speak it clarifies the issue, then I depend on you. Any dependence is lack of freedom. If you start learning, you are both the teacher and the disciple. No one needs another in this type of learning. If you need me, then I become your authority. I have been against authority from a very young age.

A disciple is one who is learning. He is learning about himself. To learn about yourself, you have to observe.

Prasad: But I have read and listened to others, and it is you that opened up the whole field.

J.K.: As long as you are aware, why are you bothered what pill cures you?

Prasad: I have gone through the whole gamut, and read so many books.

J.K.: Yes, I can see it.

Prasad: But the whole thing became clear only through you.

J.K.: But the process is in you. Others have also read the authors you read, and they also read my books. But why haven't they noticed the difference? If you have noticed it, it is because of the process in you. You are therefore the teacher and the taught, not I.

A man who observes is himself moving and is in the current.

Prasad: You then don't permit even a little image of yourself to be anywhere in our minds?

J.K.: That will only lead to dependence

Interview 4
Vasanta Vihar, Madras
January, 1984

My WIFE and I met Krishnamurti in his room at Vasanta Vihar in Adyar, Madras, and he sat near a huge window with curtains hanging down to the carpeted floor. Due to the wind outside, the curtains were moving constantly to either side. Krishnaji stopped their movement by catching hold of the loose ends. Seeing that this was an inconvenience to him, I suggested that we sit a little aside so that he need not hold the curtains. But he said "They are like that. Don't bother; carry on," and clutched them as long as he conversed with us.

One is not clear why he sometimes does not mind inconvenience to himself, and why he puts up with it. He chose to sit on a small straight-backed, armless steel chair on the dais while at Saanen, Switzerland, or at any other European gathering, and in India he chose to sit cross-legged on the dais at Rajghat, Benares, Rishi Valley, Madras, or Bangalore while giving public talks. On one occasion I asked him point blank why he invariably chose the most uncomfortable chairs. Pat came the answer, "Since I like the most uncomfortable chairs, sir." I had no reply to that.

The straight-backed chair is no doubt for keeping the spine erect. But why the lack of armrests? Perhaps that also has its own purpose. I don't know. That the dais would

69

contain no other adornment was understandable. Except for the microphone attached to his shirt, he was empty-handed, open, vulnerable, frail, and thoroughly human.

His room in Vasanta Vihar was equally plain and functional with a single bed at the far end, a small table with a notebook and some papers on it, a straight-backed wooden chair near a wall, a bookshelf with some books, and his suitcase. This was all, except for cupboards. He generally had his breakfast and lunch in the dining hall of the guest house along with a few other people.

Religious Tradition and Culture

Prasad: The religious tradition and the culture of this country are intermixed. Which part of them is worth retaining?

J.K.: May I speak frankly?

Prasad: Please do.

J.K.: I feel that neither is worth retaining. If it is tradition, it is no longer religion. Religion is not tradition. A religious mind does not come about through tradition. The religious mind is entirely new. It can have nothing to do with that which continues: so-called tradition.

As for culture, it has disappeared in India. The Indians are all after money. They worship it. The fact is that the Brahmanical tradition—I am neither supporting it nor denouncing it which has been in existence for the past three to four thousand years, has been completely wiped out. There is nothing to keep. Nothing at all.

Prasad: You want us to start afresh, on a clean slate as it were?

J.K.: Yes, start on a clean slate. Otherwise you merely repeat. The commercial motive has taken over in every sphere. Temples are the means of earning money. I am told that a temple over here collects a million rupees every three days. The other day a senior administrator who met me at Delhi was saying that someone in the south had told him that he was earning a lot of money constructing temples. Is this religion? Is this your tradition? This is either plain cynicism, or religion has become a part of the entertainment industry. Oh, what have you brought it down to?

Moral Education

Prasad: Should moral and religious education be inculcated in the young, or only observation?

J.K.: What do you mean by moral values? Suppose you have children. What will you teach them? Will you teach your child to care for his neighbor, to care for his mother and father, to care for the trees, the plants in his garden, to care for his surroundings? If there is love, care, and affection, then it is moral. But that does not exist. What exactly do you mean by moral values?

Prasad: Teach them the lives of the saints?

J.K.: The saints were not total human beings. Most of them were rather neurotic. Their development was one-sided. Teach the young the art of listening and learning, and the art of observation. If you can do that, you have taught them everything.

Teaching History

Prasad: How much and what type of history should be taught to students?

J.K.: What is history, sir? Is it the narration of what the kings did, the treasures that they grabbed, the territory that they annexed, the slaughter that they conducted? The dates of their coming into power or going out? The number of kings or queens that ruled? Is this history?

Then again, if an Indian writes it, he does it from the Indian point of view. He will naturally be prejudiced in favor of his own people. If a man from a different nation writes the same history, he does it from his own national viewpoint, from the standpoint of his own conditioning.

But history is also the story of man. And the story of man is your story.

Prasad: But at the academic level, not all the students would wish to go inward.

J.K.: That's right. Teach them the story of mankind, not my country against the others. Tell them the story of mankind and the world, and how men are broken up, how these artificial divisions as nationalities lead to war.

Root Cause

Prasad: Is there a root cause for all that is seen, for all the phenomena of this world?

J.K.:   Sir, Indians are very good at multiplying theories, very clever at this sort of thing. They then analyze those theories and make commentaries. And they have lived on commentaries. Everyone goes out to write another commentary.

The world, the human world and the world of nature, the world under water, the various species of life in the ocean, on the earth, the forests, the trees, the flowers—all this, the whole of it, has it any cause? That is your question.

From which end would you begin to understand all this? Where would you like to begin? From the point of view of human existence? Human existence and the existence of nature are interrelated. If you destroy nature, you are destroying yourself. Since we are destroying nature, we are destroying ourselves. This is a fact. We never treat existence as a whole. We never see it all together. You are asking, Is there a cause?

Prasad: Since you say that anything that has a cause must come to an end . . .

J.K.: That's right. Everything has a cause. The oak tree comes out of the acorn that has been planted. The acorn is therefore the cause of the oak tree. I eat the wrong type of food and I have a tummy ache. The deer is killed by the tiger. Turn a switch and you have light. There is cause for everything. So human beings have also a cause. We use each other for mutual benefit; we exploit each other. We do not know love.

The root cause according to the Christian faith is original sin. If you believe that, you attribute everything to it. If you believe in Allah, then you attribute it all according to your faith. But if you don't believe all that, then biologically speaking all this has arisen from the cell, the evolutionary process, man that emerged from the ape and all that.

Prasad: But is there an original cause? Not just faith but fact.

J.K.: Why do you want to know, sir. Why?

Prasad: If not, the whole drama is meaningless.

J.K.: It is meaningless as it is. You educate a child, send him or her to college. He gets a job, marries, settles down. Look at it factually. All the way up and down, it is just pleasure and sorrow.

Prasad: But someone must tell them there is a meaning.

J.K.: First see the fact. Technologically, marvelous things have been invented. We are not negating it. But see that money has become all-important. Money is power. What is the meaning of all this power and pelf? And at the end of it, what is the meaning of all this struggle, this unhappiness that we call life? It is all your making.

It has no meaning, and therefore you presume that there must be a meaning elsewhere. Since this existence has no meaning, you invent a God who originated it and who must therefore have a meaning. But that invention also has no meaning. See if there is a meaning to life here and now. See if it is meaningful, and then you will know the answer. As long as thought is in operation, nothing has any meaning.

Where Is Intelligence Found?

Prasad: You say that intelligence is everywhere and that it does not abide in one's heart and mind. Tradition says that intelligence, while being everywhere, resides mostly in the hearts of good men. Your comment please.

J.K.: What is intelligence? It is assumed that one needs intelligence to go to the moon or to build a car. But real intelligence is not cleverness; it is not intellection; it is not put together by thought. But all the activity of thought, of going to the moon, the development of rapid communication, and also the fact that each man is out for himself, is treated as intelligence. We also use the term in respect to the wars that we conduct. But all this is merely the activity of thought, the gathering of a tremendous amount of knowledge, not intelligence.

So what is intelligence? The word "intelligence" comes from Latin. It means to gather information, to read between the lines, and to act correctly on the basis of the information gathered. I say that intelligence is also love and compassion. Such intelligence is not the product of thought or time.

Your question is also about intelligence residing in the hearts of good men. Sir, who is a good man? Do I know that I am a good man? If I know it, would I be a good man?

Prasad: But we know you.

J.K.: How do you know that I am good unless you are good yourself? And if you are not, how would you know it? How does one recognize?

78

Functioning of the Senses

Prasad: You suggest that the senses should all operate at their highest level. Can you kindly elaborate? At their highest level, do the senses have only a greater intensity, or do they acquire a totally different quality?

J.K.: Scientists say that the brain is fragmented into the left and the right. We do not know the activity of the total brain, a brain that is not fragmented. The brain is the center of all the senses. As it is, we function with only one or two senses. We really don't know the state when all the senses are fully awakened and when they all function together at the highest level. Human beings know only how to function in a fragmented manner. When the brain functions without this fragmentation, when all the senses are awakened, the self disappears totally, and the brain then has a different quality, a different energy.

Role of Experience in Seeking Truth

Prasad: What is experience? Does it have any role in knowing the Truth? Does one get the experiences one has invariably wished for?

J.K.: Now, what is experience? The experience of sex, the experience of going to the moon, a car accident. Walking down the street, I see a poor dog; that also is an experience. That experience has become knowledge. And that knowledge gives me security.

Does experience have any role in knowing the truth? Certainly not. No role at all. Truth is not knowledge. It cannot be recognized and therefore cannot be experienced.

The next part of your question is whether one gets the experience that one has wished for. Of course, I create my experience. If I want to experience drunkenness, I get drunk. If I wish to experience something else, I get it.

Prasad: Do I get what I deserve?

J.K.: No, not what you deserve, but what you desire.

Religious Conversions

Prasad: In the context of aggressive conversion, Hinduism appears to have been thrown on the defensive, and it is organizing itself. But sometimes this also seems to take the offensive. Your comment please.

J.K.: To me, all the religious organizations, be they Christian, Hindu, Buddhist, or any other, have nothing to do with true religion. Suppose I believe in some form of a religious concept and I want to convert you. If I have my religion only for myself, I feel lonely, I feel lost. Hinduism says one thing and Islam another, and therefore they wage a holy war, a jihad; they convert and use force. If someone is dogmatic, he wants to convert everyone around him. In order to meet this aggressive spirit, this onslaught, the Hindu also becomes aggressive. One aggression tries to counter the other.

But all this is based upon opinion, dogma, fixed belief, and the sacred books. No book on earth is holy. Once everyone accepts that we are human beings and not mere labels such as the Hindu, the Muslim, and the Christian, and one sees that we are conditioned through religious propaganda, then there will be a total change. As long as this conditioning based on propaganda, fear, and belief exists, there will be divisions, there will be wars, and they will be called defensive.

I say to you, don't be a Hindu, don't be a Muslim, don't be a national. But you never give up any of these things. It is silly and unintelligent to hold on to these divisions. Both sides are seeking security, but there is no

security when you are divided on the basis of
your opinion. See the stupidity of it.

Science and Technology

Prasad: Western society has developed science and technology and appears to be on the brink of destroying itself. Some rethinking appears to be going on over there. Here in India we have not progressed in science and technology greatly. Considering the experience of the West, what would be your advice to Indians?

J.K.: The scientists say that if there is a nuclear war the whole world will be destroyed. Not the Western world only—the whole world. In this country you have nuclear development also. It is no longer a question of the West or East. There is no Western thought and Eastern thought. There is only man and his thought, and he is destroying himself. But man doesn't see that he is bringing destruction on himself.

You want to know what advice I would give to Indians. Advice is given by fools only. But look at the fact that Western technology has entered into the Eastern world. It is technology that has taken over everywhere, not Western or Eastern. Certainly it is the West that

has invented the atom bomb, but it has also
invented rapid communication, made tremendous advances in medicine, and these are also
taking place in India. Technology is necessary. You wouldn't be here to meet with me if
you had traveled by bullock cart. Without
advances in medicine, disease would be ram-
pant.

But technology is also responsible for the great
instruments of war that it has produced.
Technology has proved that it can do good
and also do harm. So what is important is not
the ending of technology, but the changing of
the human consciousness which uses this technology.

We human beings are all one. We are humanity. If we destroy one human being, we are
destroying ourselves.

Interview 5
Rishi Valley
December, 1984

THE VENUE for the interview this time was Rishi Valley School, and the meeting place was Krishnamurti's room, located on the first floor of the old guest house where he stays for a short period every year. It is sparsely furnished in a manner similar to his room in Vasanta Vihar.

It is said that a bird once visited this room and started tapping on the windowpane. Krishnaji murmured to it softly, "I can allow you inside now. But after I leave this place, they will close the room, and you will not be able to stay here. So I'm sorry." Was the bird tapping to enter the room and stay? Krishnamurti understood it that way. Can there be silent communication between human beings and other forms of life?

Krishnamurti used to speak softly to non-human creatures, including trees. It is said that he once spoke in a mango grove to a couple of trees that did not bear fruit, alerting them that the management was thinking of cutting them down. Krishnaji disclaims all further responsibility for what happened thereafter, but the two trees did bear fruit during that season!

Right Education

Prasad: How is one to enable the young to discover their real purpose in life?

J.K.: When they are very young, they will not be able to find out. But look at what the parents do to the children. Parents want them to find a good job, get married, and settle down. Society and their surroundings are so very corrupt. The children are put in such a dreadful position that when they grow up they are always worried about their employment, their future, marriage, and bad government. These absorb the young. They can only follow the traditional pattern, caught in this maelstrom. How will they find the real purpose? At that age I don't think they will be able to find out.

Everything, therefore, depends on proper education at that age. But you have a lopsided society. People don't want to work with their hands in this country. We once offered a plot of one hundred acres to a number of young men, along with the necessary facilities to cultivate it. They were not willing to take it because it would soil their hands. I once grew vegetables, milked the cows in the mountains of California and learned to do everything myself, including my own cooking. The young do not even know how to cook for themselves.

In this type of society, how do you expect
them to discover the real purpose in life?
They will first have to be educated rightly.

Knowing: Loving

Prasad: What is knowing? Is it experiencing
or realizing?

J.K.: What does the word mean to you?
(Looks out of the window and points his
finger.) There is a flower. I know it botan-
ically, how it grows and all that. But that is
only a small part of the flower. I do not really
know it, know the whole of it; I only see it.
I have been meeting you or your daughter
during the last few years, but do I know you?
I know you only partly. I can never say that I
know about a living thing completely. It is
growing, moving. When I say I know you,
there is a division. I can never know you
fully. All knowing is partial.

Prasad: Is it because a living thing is unpredictable?

J.K.: Yes, unpredictable, changing, moving. Go a little further into it. What relationship has knowledge with love? Love is not
knowledge.

Prasad: But one might like to have some knowledge of that which is loved?

J.K.: Knowledge is based on experience, on a great deal of memory, recorded by the brain. Is love knowledge? Knowledge is thought, part of thought. Love is not the result of thought. Love is not pleasure, not desire. I do not love you because you give me pleasure or money. All that is calculation.

All knowledge is additive. It is essentially based on experience. You create a hypothesis, test it, throw it out, test another, and thus accumulate knowledge. Therefore, knowledge is always limited, either now or in the future.

What is realizing? Let us say that I do not know how to drive a car. I do not know what a car is. I dismantle it and then put it together. I learn about it and at the end I realize that I can drive a car. But it is still knowledge and capacity.

Our brain is the center of all responses, sensations, reactions, and pleasure, which are all in the field of thought. How can love be there? It must be outside of thought, not inside. The mind is different from the brain; the mind is outside the brain.

That Which Knows

Prasad: What is it that knows? I see that it is neither the intellect nor the emotions. Is it a case of the intelligence within one knowing the intelligence outside?

J.K.:   What do you mean by that word "intelligence"?

Prasad: Other than the intellect and the emotions, there must be something that grasps what you are talking about.

J.K.:   First of all, let us be clear about this word. Intelligence, as it is understood, is the capacity to gather information, distinguish, analyze, and rationalize. There is the intelligence of thought. Thought is capable of building a house or a car, of putting a man on the moon. Thought has worked out all this, the whole of this technological world. That intelligence of thought is limited, as thought itself is limited. Intellectually, I may be very clear, but emotionally I may be totally confused.

The brain is the seat of this intelligence. Therefore, it can imagine the ultimate, Brahman, and it can attribute many things to it. But it is still born of thought. Is the person— me, my name, my qualities—different from the brain? Brain is matter, and thought is a material process which creates its own intelligence.

There is a different kind of intelligence which is not limited, which is outside the brain. There is an intelligence of love and compassion which has nothing to do with thought.

The Flower and Its Perfume

Prasad: It has been said that he who knows does not speak and he who speaks does not know. But you know and also speak. Perhaps the speaking is mechanical and the knowing nonmechanical. Is this true when you do these two things simultaneously?

J.K.: Can we put it very simply? See that jasmine flower outside the window. It has an extraordinary scent. The scent is the speech of that flower. You cannot separate them. The scent is not different from that flower.

Tapping the Potential

Prasad: When one reads between the lines of what you have spoken, a lot is revealed. But I am sure you have a lot more which has not been tapped. How do we get at it?

J.K.: When we dig a well, we go to a certain depth and there is water. Most people are satisfied with that little water. That little water might evaporate on account of the heat of the sun. You have to dig deeper for a permanent water source. You have to have the capacity to dig deep. It depends on you.

Prasad: We have to do a lot of homework.

J.K.: Yes, and when you do the homework, the digging, it is not the well that gives you more water. It is your homework, your digging, that gives you the water.

Rhythm of the Brain and the Universe

Prasad: You have often said that the brain has its own rhythm. The universe also has its own rhythm. Are these coterminous?

J.K.: When you are very quiet, when there is no activity of thought and you are breathing and your nerves are alive, you can see that the brain has its own movement, its own rhythm. The universe is in perfect order. The sun rises at a certain time; the new moon and full moon occur at certain times. The whole universe, with its black holes . . .

Prasad: Including the volcanoes . . .

J.K.: Yes, everything. The whole universe is in perfect order. But man is not. When man is quiet, there is the biological rhythm, the phenomenon of breathing. But our thought creates disorder. Our consciousness is in perpetual conflict with its ambition and greed. It is in a flux, a state of disorder. When there is real order, not induced order, then that order is the universe.

Woman and Spiritual Knowledge

Prasad: Tradition says that woman is not as fit for receiving spiritual knowledge as man. In understanding you and in being able to live according to your teachings, do you notice any difference between man and woman?

J.K.: No, sir. Woman has certain biological troubles. She has to bear children. She has to be much more sensitive. She has to have security to bear and bring up the child. When the child is born, her concern is the baby. She has to think only of the child for the first five years.

Man has his own difficulties. He has to earn a living. He has to protect the family. Knowing this difference, knowing woman's incapacity during certain periods, knowing what she is doing, and not getting caught in it—that is

94

M. A. Hamid, Rishi Valley, India

important. Then what is the difference between man and the woman? In fact, woman is much more sensitive than man. She is less selfish.

Prasad: But while trying to protect the family and the children, she is more selfish?

J.K.: She may be protectively selfish, but selfless also. Both man and woman have their own pressure and trouble. But the important point is not to get caught, not to get trapped by this.

Easterner and Westerner

Prasad: True, you do not recognize nationalities. But can you tell us if there is any difference between the Easterner and the Westerner responding to you with their respective backgrounds?

J.K.: The Indian brain has studied philosophy. The Indians are a much older people—more than three to five thousand years old. There was a special group among them, the Brahmins, who cultivated their brains. To them, knowledge was important, learning was important, and so-called spiritual life was important. They may not live it. But they are quick at capturing it with the intellect, quick

in analyzing, explaining, but not in acting on
it. If my observation is correct, they do not
relate their intellectual perception to their
daily activity.

Prasad: There is total divorce between the
seeing and acting.

J.K.:   I won't call it hypocrisy, but they are
not religious. The Westerner is more skep-
tical, argumentative. But when he gets something into him, even if he gets it slowly, he
does it. In the cold climate in which he lives,
he has to be up and doing. He has to dig and
work. He can't sit back and indulge in endless
analysis, which is possible in India with its
monsoons. During the rainy season, for a few
months in the year people can't work in the
open. Perhaps the difference between the
Easterner and the Westerner has something to
do with the climate.

Religious Propaganda

Prasad: The spread of religion or faith is
through compromise with the local situation.
It can then become a mass movement. Not so
the teachings of Krishnamurti which, being
the inner core of religion, do not permit any
compromise. Necessarily, they have to be confined to a few understanding groups. How do

we solve this difficulty in spreading the teaching?

J.K.:   Let us differentiate between propaganda and the man who is living it.

Prasad: Which means the living is the teaching.

J.K.:   If I am doing propaganda, repeating what somebody has said, then I compromise. Take Christianity. Christ's teachings were recorded after sixty-three years. You can well imagine how much of it could be accurate. And then they do propaganda. I say it is not a question of propaganda, but a question of living it.

I have always said ''no help'' to another in this direction. The Buddha said no help but the Buddhists began preaching, thus destroying what the Buddha said. What happened to Christ's teaching happened to Buddha's teaching also. The followers have destroyed it by doing propaganda.

The important thing is living the teaching, and not spreading it. You were there in the hall when we were talking as a group. [Here Krishnamurti refers to a group of teachers of the Rishi Valley and the Bangalore Valley Schools.] If those fifty people in the hall lived it . . .

Prasad: It would spread of its own accord.

J.K.: One person can change the consciousness of men, if he lives it. Propaganda, to me,
is really a process of destroying the truth.

Withdrawal

Prasad: Did you at any time feel the urge to
completely withdraw? If so, what prompted
you to remain here and speak?

J.K.: I have felt it very often. I think, sir,
when fairly sensitive people, those who feel
strongly about things, see so much violence
they react by saying, ''For god's sake, I won't
have anything to do with this.''

Prasad: One would like to simply walk out
of the whole thing.

J.K.: But what is the use of such with-
drawal? The monk or saint who withdraws is
still caught in his ritual. He is still committed
to a dogma. He is not completely detached.

Prasad: You continue to live with us,
though you sometimes see the futility of it.

J.K.: But I never expect anything. I am
neither elated nor depressed, whether it is two

thousand or only two who come to listen to me. Total detachment. That is real Sanyasa.

Interview 6
Vasanta Vihar, Madras
December, 1985

THE AIR was thick with rumors that Krishnaji was not well and that he had canceled his Bombay talks to fly back to Los Angeles directly from Madras. There was a certain gravity and sadness all around. But Krishnaji was his usual self when my wife and I met him in his room on the first floor of Vasanta Vihar.

I knew that we were putting a strain on him by attempting to interview him, and I told him at the very outset that I would not like to trouble him if he did not feel like it. He said, "Don't bother, go ahead." I offered to read my typewritten questions this time, instead of putting the sheet before him as in other years. "Do it any way you choose," he replied.

I could see that he was a bit weary. Just prior to my meeting, a Quaker woman from Europe met with him for a brief time. I was, perhaps, the last Indian representative of a news weekly to meet him before he left on his final journey to the United States.

All along I had entertained a strong desire to bow deeply to Krishnaji in the traditional Indian manner, but I also knew Krishnaji's reluctance, if not aversion, to that manner of salutation. He had revealed to a close associate at one time that if someone touched his feet, he would be obliged to touch the other person's feet in return. To Krishnaji, literally every human being partakes of the sacred!

On a different occasion when I stood in a deferential manner while expressing my gratefulness to him for some kindness on his part, he "pulled me up" by remarking, "You need not bow to me, sir. You may do it elsewhere, not here. We are old friends."

But I could not get rid of my desire to bow to him in reverence at least once in my life. Therefore, after the interview was over, while all three of us were seated on the floor cross-legged, I hesitantly sought his permission to bow to him. "Oh no, sir," responded Krishnaji smilingly. Instead, he swiftly bowed his head to the ground from his sitting position. My wife and I were taken aback, we stood up and folded our hands in salutation. Krishnaji moved away to a small table near the wall and stood there with his back to us, allowing us to move away from the room. Normally he would have stood at the door of his room to see us off. But this time our suggestion about bowing to him seemed to have affected him. He had said elsewhere, "Too much devotion is bad for me." I wonder whether we did the right thing in attempting to bow to him on that occasion.

Self-Centeredness

Prasad: The self-preservation instinct in man leads to selfishness in every field of activity. How does one avoid the trap?

J.K.: Why is there such emphasis on self-interest, on a separate soul, separate ego, separate personality? The whole social structure encourages self-interest. This has been one of the problems throughout history—how to bring about a society in which self-interest does not predominate. Religions, sects, and gurus have tried everything. But possibly the gurus themselves were self-interested. I don't think any society, leader, or guru has tried to stop it; they have encouraged it.

Prasad: Perhaps in the larger interest of the group or nation?

J.K.: Yes, the so-called larger interest, which is, however, really not so. Their self-interest is given a different name.

You want to know how one can avoid this self-interest. Well, each one has to have a certain way of looking at life, at how this self-interest arises in oneself, what shape it takes, under what cloak it hides. All this has to be be found out.

M. A. Hamid, Rishi Valley, India

Prasad: You would like the whole thing to be looked at in a scientific, impersonal way.

Conformity

Prasad: I understand that initiation and conformity come by way of "seeing." But you categorize them under "violence." How?

J.K.: A man conforms. He is put into a straightjacket. This is violence. He tries to fit into society. But society has use only for engineers or politicians. He then tries to be one, by approximating himself to the demands of that society. This produces conflict in him. The politician has to do what the people demand of him, right or wrong. Is all this not violence to the individual and to society?

Terrorism

Prasad: Nationalism is bad enough, but of late, subnationalism is also rearing its head, using terrorism to attain its goal. Your comment please.

J.K.: What is the purpose of a terrorist, sir? It's purpose is to make you feel terrified. Terror is a means of getting what one wants by holding someone hostage, putting fear into everyone by killing.

Why do I join a terrorist organization? Because I want to achieve an end which the opposition won't allow me to achieve in the normal course. I want to push my ideas on other people when I cannot convince them.

Russian Ban on Krishnamurti's Books

Prasad: Your books are said to be banned in Soviet Russia, though the authorities seem to tolerate religious books of various denominations. Why do they fear you more?*

J.K.:   I am aware of the ban. They permit the religious books because those books are harmless. So far as my books are concerned, I don't think it is fear. Their reluctance is because Krishnamurti talks a great deal about freedom, and they are naturally against it. There is an old joke you have probably heard:

A Soviet drunk goes into Red Square and starts shouting "Brezhnev is a fool" at the top of his voice. The Soviet police arrest him and haul him up before a magistrate. The magis-

---

* Krishnamurti's books are now available in Russian in the U.S.S.R.—ED.

trate listens to the charge and sentences the drunk to a period of twenty-two years in jail. The man pleads, "I can understand a two year sentence for the offense that I committed. But why such a heavy sentence?" The magistrate replies, "What you say is right. Your sentence is two years for the drunken misbehavior in a public place; the other twenty is for revealing a state secret."

Prasad: But there is so much clarity and light in all that you state.

J.K.: They don't want it. They want their system to work, the system that evolved from their grandfathers' period.

Human Mind in the Twenty-First Century

Prasad: Everyone is talking of the Indian entering the twenty-first century. Apart from the material planning that is being done in this direction, what type of a mind would be needed for grappling with the problems of this country and the world?

J.K.: The problems of this country are many. Immense poverty and overpopulation. The government is unable to do much in regard to these problems. Also we are entering into the computer world, and the computer can out-think man. It can do almost everything that the human brain can do. The computer can even think backwards and forwards. Then what will happen to the human brain? Will it begin to wither?

And what is our educational system? Are we educating our children to become just good technicians, to get good pay and perks, and then to settle down for a life of pleasure? If education does not teach you to observe life and understand it, of what use is education?

You come and speak to me every year and then publish it. Does anyone read all this?

Prasad: Some do. Those who are earnest.

J.K.:   But they don't pay attention to what is said. No, sir, no one wants to learn.

The Last Bow

Krishnamurti's last public talk in Madras was delivered on the evening of January 4, 1986, and we all attended. On the next day, January 5, the teachers of Rishi Valley School took leave of Krishnaji in the afternoon. My wife and I joined the teachers standing around and saying good-bye.

I emerged from behind the group and moved towards Krishnamurti. He laughed and said, "Hey, I thought you were hiding behind the others." I asked, "May I hold your hands?" "Yes," he replied and held mine. My wife tells me that I bowed my head deeply and touched his clasping hands with my head, though I was not wholly conscious of what I was doing at that moment.

Later, Krishnaji left the country for California, and according to the Indian calendar, he passed away on February 17, 1986. The authorities of the All Indian Radio in Hyderabad suggested that I speak about Krishnaji in Telugu, and I paid homage to him in a broadcast at 7:45 P.M. on February 18, 1986.

Epilogue

Krishnamurti in the Modern Context

SOME YEARS have passed since Krishnamurti died in February, 1986, at the ripe old age of ninety-one. Naturally people would like to know how relevant his message is to today's fast-moving life, which does not appear to have a sense of direction.

We are witnessing at present among all the nations of the world, irrespective of the Iron and Bamboo Curtains, a tremendous hunger for freedom and the tearing down of the bastions of authority. But man is conditioned to think only in terms of political, social, and economic freedoms, which are all of a limited character. He does not know what it is to reject all authority and be really free and unbound. Also he does not know that this is the absolute illimitable freedom that he is really thirsting for, all other freedoms being a distortion of this real freedom. So long as the urge for freedom springs in the human heart, Krishnamurti will continue to be relevant. For did he not, very early in his life, declare

113

emphatically that he was determined "to set man unconditionally free"?

Typically, modern man has no belief in anything. He is not willing to believe that there is a god whom he is unable to see with his physical eyes. Neither does he believe in a heaven or hell of which he has no direct experience. With this disbelief goes overboard the so-called morality and good conduct which man adopted through fear of consequences in bygone ages.

In addition, it is difficult to convince man that the world of so-called reality is only real in the apparent sense of the word, and even what he treats as physical reality is only an assemblage of atoms and molecules arranged in a certain order. So man believes what he can see and feel for himself, for "seeing is believing." It is important that he be made to "see" before he can believe or trust and know for himself. Traditional religion, which ask for belief and faith long before man can really see, are not capable of meeting modern man's need at this juncture. In my view Krishnamurti alone can meet this need fully.

Krishnamurti has always considered that the man who says that he believes and the man who declares that he does not believe are sailing in the same boat. The believer who swears by the apparent reality is no more sure

114

of such a reality than is the disbeliever. For all that we know, both of them could be equally right or equally wrong. Krishnamurti has a simple solution for this dilemma. He says, "Don't believe anything handed down to you by authority, however hoary or ancient it may be." Doubt it.

Doubt a thing even after you reach an advanced stage in your development. It is necessary to doubt even your initial experience and test it. You are then empty, void of all worldly conditioning. This is the state of the great unknowing, the great innocence, when real knowledge can be born. One comes to know with a strange certainty beyond all shadow of doubt, and with that certainty arises a sense of responsibility to the whole of creation.

But another person's certainty is not your certainty, just as the satiation of another's hunger does not satisfy yours. You have to doubt the believer and deny the unbeliever equally. Belief and disbelief are both of the mind, while the heart alone can truly know. You have to discover for yourself whether there is a higher reality. In this process you watch yourself carefully while your conditioning is unfolding every day. Since such watching or awareness is the only available instrument to man, and available to each and every person irrespective of one's station in life, everyone can pick it up and use it. The nature of one's likes, opinions, attachments, prejudices, strong and weak points, illusions, and all that constitutes one's conditioning will be thrown up to the surface. Through the process of awareness when all these wither and drop away, one becomes really free. To such a free person any situation will reveal what urgently needs to be done, and it gets done through that person spontaneously, automatically, without any premeditation. Such action arising on the spur of the moment is uncontaminated and free. It does not belong to any one person and cannot therefore be appropriated by anyone.

In this way a process of insightful seeing and acting comes into operation, which goes on as long as life continues. Action arising from such a pure insight is unsullied, wise, and liberating. In this modern age, when organized religions and cults strongly anchored on belief and faith are crumbling everywhere, Krishnamurti is the answer.

About the Author

N. Lakshmi Prasad, a graduate in Economics from the Madras University in India, was Director, Bureau of Economics and Statistics, for the Government of Añdhra Pradesh, Hyderabad. Interested in religion and philosophy for many years and familiar with the teachings of Theosophy, Sufism, Zen Masters, Meher Baba, Gurdjieff and Ouspensky, he has written articles for journals and periodicals, mostly in Telugu and occasionally in English. He has been a weekly columnist for two news dailies in Telugu and has broadcast talks on technical and philosophic subjects over the All India Radio, Hyderabad. At the request of the radio authorities, the day after J. Krishnamurti's death he broadcast a talk paying homage to him.

QUEST BOOKS
are published by
The Theosophical Society in America,
Wheaton, Illinois 60189-0270,
a branch of a world organization
dedicated to the promotion of the unity of
humanity and the encouragement of the study of
religion, philosophy, and science, to the end that
we may better understand ourselves and our place in
the universe. The Society stands for complete
freedom of individual search and belief.
In the Classics Series well-known
theosophical works are made
available in popular editions.
For more information
write or call.
1-708-668-1571